The Cl
Sand Castle Key

By Joan Hiatt Harlow
Illustrated by Fiona King

www.WrightGroup.com

Wright Group

The Creatures of Sand Castle Key

Text by Joan Hiatt Harlow
Illustrations by Fiona King

Printed in China through Colorcraft Ltd., Hong Kong

Send all inquiries to:
Wright Group/McGraw-Hill
P.O. Box 812960
Chicago, IL 60681

ISBN 0-322-04502-9
ISBN 0-322-04598-3 (6-pack)

6 7 8 9 10 11 12 13 CC 10 09 08 07 06 05 04

The McGraw·Hill Companies

Contents

CHAPTER 1
Creepy Creatures!

My two-week spring break in Florida didn't start out too well. Who wants to do a homework assignment on vacation? Not me. I had been grumbling all morning. But after missing a week of school with the flu, I had some catching up to do. Grandma said, "Get your project done, Joshua. Then you'll have it off your mind."

Before I started to work on that project, I just *had* to see my friends, the Geckos. We live in different places, but on school vacations we all come to visit our grandparents at their retirement park in Venetia. Maybe we'd find a new mystery to solve!

Last year, we started a detective club. We named it The Geckos, after the little lizards that dart in and out of the rocks and bushes. They have sticky pads on their feet so they can climb up walls and peek out from around corners. It's a perfect name for a detective club. There are five of us in the club. There's me, Joshua Jacy from Oklahoma. Then there's my best Florida friend, Tim Taylor from New Hampshire. The rest are girls—the Alexander twins, Denise and Melissa, from New York City, and last, but by no means least, is Cassandra Kelly from California. We call her Cassie.

After breakfast the Geckos met at the pool. It was a sunny, warm day and the palm branches were clicking in the breeze. Tim looked bigger this year. "I've been eating too much of the candy that I'm supposed to be selling for our baseball team," he said.

Cassie was as cute as ever, with her reddish gold hair and kind of turned-up nose. But she had a cast on her left arm. "How did you do that?" I asked.

"Skiing." Cassie looked kind of sad. "I can't swim while I'm in this plaster cast." Then she brightened. "I'm seeing the doctor here on Friday, and he may remove it. I hope so. It's hot and itchy."

I thought about Cassie with her broken arm. She couldn't swim and her cast was uncomfortable. I felt guilty. I shouldn't be complaining about doing a homework assignment. I could still go swimming and have fun.

"Any ideas for my science project?" I asked the Geckos.

No one answered. It was hard to think about schoolwork when a blue swimming pool glimmered in front of us.

"I did a huge project on my family's heritage," I told my friends. "I learned a lot about my family and my people, the Seminole Indians. And I got an A plus. I would think one big project a year is enough."

"But that wasn't science," Melissa said. "That must have been social studies."

"You're right," I said. "It *was* for my social studies class."

Melissa and her twin, Denise, look and dress exactly alike. When we had trouble figuring out who was who, they decided to wear different-colored headbands. Melissa wears hot pink, and Denise wears bright yellow. Those two are so much alike they're always finishing each other's sentences.

"I have no idea what to do for a science project," I said. "My teacher said we could select any science topic we wanted, but I don't have a clue what to choose."

"I know!" Cassie shouted. *"Paleontology!"*

"Paleontology?" I asked. "What's that?"

"Fossils," said Cassie. "The study of fossils."

"You're kidding," I said.

"No, I'm not kidding. The beaches here in Venetia have lots of fossils." Cassie's blue eyes sparkled. "We can go to the beach and spend the whole afternoon collecting fossils for your science project."

"Let's do it!" said Melissa. "It would be..."

"...fun!" Denise said.

That very afternoon the five of us met in

the shade under the beach pavilion out on Manasota Key. Then off we went to find fossils on the beach. We each had a plastic pail for our specimens.

"You'll need to get a book at the library to help you identify the rocks we find," Cassie suggested.

"Rocks?" Tim asked. "I thought we were finding fossils."

Cassie rolled her eyes. "The fossils here *are* rocks. They've become *petrified,* Tim. They've turned to stone."

"I knew that," Tim muttered, looking away.

"But not all fossils are petrified," Cassie went on. "In California, where I live, there are tar pits full of fossils—like mammoths and saber-toothed cats, all preserved in tar."

"Don't forget amber," said Denise.

"What's amber?" I asked.

"It's hardened sap from ancient trees. Bugs are preserved in amber," replied Melissa.

"This beach has been picked over," said Denise, after we had searched a while and only found a few sharks' teeth.

"Maybe we should go down to Sand Castle Key," said Tim. "No one ever goes out on that island."

"You won't get *us* out there," Denise said quickly.

Her sister nodded. "We've heard stories about Sand Castle Key."

"What stories?" I asked.

"I've heard those silly rumors, too," said Cassie. "But I don't believe them. Not for one minute."

"What rumors?" I asked again.

"Our grandparents saw lights out there," said Denise.

"What lights?" I demanded.

"My grandparents don't believe there's a creature out there. Do yours?" asked Tim.

"Hello! Does anyone hear me?" I yelled. "What creature? Will someone please tell me what's going on?"

"Sand Castle Key is a deserted island," Denise explained. "There's no electricity or people or anything out there. Just an old fishing shack."

"But recently people have seen lights very late at night," Melissa said.

Denise's eyes were huge. "And they say there's a creature that crawls up on the sand."

"What kind of creature?" I asked. This was becoming interesting.

"A sea creature," Melissa whispered.

I had goose bumps on my arms. We all looked at one another silently for a moment.

Then I said, "This sounds like a mystery for the Geckos!"

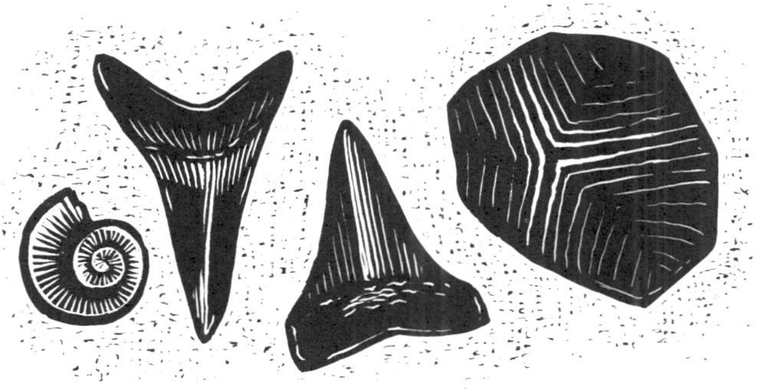

CHAPTER 2

Sharks' Teeth and Shells

"Yes!" Tim agreed. "Let's go out to Sand Castle Key."

"But how? Isn't it an island?" I asked.

"It is now," Cassie explained. "What's now Sand Castle Key was part of Manasota Key until Hurricane Betsy swept in two years ago. It eroded Manasota Key so much that it actually became separated into two keys."

"Why do they call these islands keys?" Tim asked.

"My grandma told me it comes from the Spanish word *cayo,*" Melissa said.

"That means 'small island'," Denise added. "The Spanish were the first to settle here."

"No," I said. "Indians were here first."

"Who got to name the new island?" Tim asked.

"People started calling it Sand Castle Key because its sand dunes make the island look like a castle. The water that separates Sand Castle Key from Manasota Key is called 'the moat'," said Melissa.

"When the tide is low, the water in 'the moat' is only up to your ankles," said Cassie. "I went across it with my grandma last year."

"Did you see any creatures?" Tim kidded.

"Only the kind of creatures that Josh is looking for," Cassie said with a grin at me. "Creatures from the past."

We put on our sandals. No telling what the walking would be like out on the deserted island, since the beach had eroded.

It took about a half hour to reach the end of Manasota Key and what was now a trickle of water that separated the two islands. We took off our sandals and put them in our pails.

"See? It's only ankle deep." Cassie led the way, as usual. "The tide is out."

In no time we had crossed through the moat and were standing on Sand Castle Key.

"Let's get to work," said Tim. "A pail full of fossils ought to be enough for Joshua's project. Then we can concentrate on our new mystery."

"This *is* fun," Melissa said. "It doesn't seem like doing homework at all."

"Melissa and I will do the side of the island that overlooks the bay," said Denise. The twins headed over the dune and disappeared from sight.

"You do the shore by the gulf," Cassie said to Tim.

"All by myself?"

"Don't tell me you're worried about those stupid creatures," Cassie teased.

"No, of course not!" Tim stomped off toward the water.

"Come on, Josh. You and I will check out the old road." Cassie was already running up the embankment where the old road had been. The tar was filling with weeds and the edges were washing away with each storm.

From here, we could see both sides of the narrow island. On one side, the twins were examining a fossil. On the other side, Tim was kneeling on the sand, checking out something. Far out on the water was a boat that seemed to be anchored there. Fishermen, probably.

Cassie plunked one rock after another into her pail. "All these black rocks are petrified bones or teeth."

"My dad's a dentist," I told her.

"So?"

"He says tooth enamel is the strongest part of our bodies. Maybe that's why they petrify so well," I replied.

I saw something sharp jutting out from under the crumbling tar and pulled it out. "Take a look at this shark's tooth, Cassie. It's the biggest one yet."

"It must be three inches long," said Cassie.

"See where it's shiny? Maybe that's where the enamel was. I wonder how old it is."

"Probably a gazillion years or more. That's a beauty, Josh."

I put the shark's tooth in my pail carefully.

"I hope we find different kinds of fossils," I said. "Not just teeth."

"Here's something interesting." Cassie handed me a flat stone. "I think this is a turtle or tortoise shell. See the pretty markings?"

I placed it into my pail. Then I stood up and looked out at the aqua blue Gulf of Mexico. A pelican glided solemnly by as if it were patrolling the island.

Cassie pointed to the banks of sand. "Some of these mounds are not sand dunes. They're piles of shells."

"Indian middens," I explained. "My grandfather says this is where our ancestors cleaned shellfish long ago."

Just then, Tim came running up the embankment waving his hands. His face was red with excitement.

"Come see what I found on the sand!" he yelled. "There really is a creature on Sand Castle Key!"

CHAPTER 3
An Ancient Coin

Cassie signaled to the twins, and we all followed Tim down to the water's edge.

"Look at these big tracks!" Tim said breathlessly. "Whatever made them is not human."

The tracks looked like some creature with fins and claws had dragged itself out of the water and onto the hard sand. We followed the grotesque tracks up onto the shells of the midden, where they disappeared, leaving only a trace of a path.

Melissa grabbed her sister's hand. "That does it! Josh has enough fossils. Let's get out of here."

We all nodded. Just as we started to run toward the moat, I saw a black coin among the shells. I picked it up and put it deep in my pocket and then raced after my friends.

The water that separated the islands was almost up to our knees so we held our pails up high and waded to the other side.

On the sand a blonde woman in white knee-length pants and a bright blue shirt was watching us. When we got near her, she smiled and said, "My goodness, you're a brave group. I didn't think anyone dared to go to Sand Castle Key with all the talk about the creatures out there."

We looked at one another. Should we tell this lady what we saw? Then Cassie said, "We didn't see any creatures."

It was true. We only saw those scary tracks.

"I've heard that something comes out of the water onto the shore." The woman's voice lowered. "Something that's not human."

"Do you really believe those stories?" Denise asked.

"I heard it from a very reliable source. If I were you, I'd stay away from that island." The lady wasn't smiling now. "It might be very dangerous. There could be many sea creatures that we don't even know about."

Melissa nodded. "My grandfather is from South Africa. When he was a little boy, a fisherman caught a sea creature that everyone thought was extinct."

"Yes, I've heard of that," the lady said. "It was a coelacanth. No one believed there were still some living. Since then they've found

more in the Indian Ocean." She gave us each a warning look. "See? There *are* things out there—"

"But that turned out to be just a rare fish, not some big, scary sea creature," Denise interrupted.

"Not so many years ago, some men sailed a raft called the Kon Tiki across the Pacific Ocean. They encountered strange creatures never seen before or since." The woman spoke in a whisper that gave me chills. "The sea is full of mysteries."

"We probably won't be going back," I told her. "We were collecting fossils for my science project." I held out my pail that was half filled with black stones. "We have quite a few."

"Oh, that's good. Now you don't need to go out there again." The lady looked relieved.

We all waved and headed back to the pavilion. When we were beyond the woman's hearing, Denise whispered, "She seemed really worried about us being out there."

"And she knew all about the coelacanth," said Melissa.

"She seems to be pretty smart," Cassie said. "I can't believe she thinks those stories about the sea creatures on Sand Castle Key are true."

"Maybe we'd better stay away from that island," said Tim.

"When you see what I found, you'll want to go back." I stopped and pulled the black coin from my pocket. "I think this is from a pirate's ship."

Everyone crowded around me and stared at the black disk in my palm.

"No way!" Tim said doubtfully. "Pirates have gold. This doesn't look like gold to me."

"It's *silver,*" said Cassie. "Silver tarnishes. Look! There are some markings on it." She pointed to the faint outline of a cross. "I think Josh is right. This does look like an old Spanish coin."

"Now I want to go back tomorrow and look for more," I exclaimed.

Tim and Cassie were excited, too, but the twins were nervous. "What about those awful tracks on the sand?" Melissa asked.

"And the warning that lady gave us?" Denise added.

"Don't be such little 'fraidy cats," Cassie scolded.

"We should keep this a secret," Tim said. "Or everyone will be out there on Sand Castle Key looking for treasure."

"It's getting late," I said. "I've got to get a book about fossils at the library before it closes. Then let's show this coin to my grandfather. He might know something about it."

"We can't tell anyone else," Tim said.

I put the coin back in my pocket and turned to look at the mysterious island.

The lady was still standing near the moat with her arms crossed, watching us. She looked as if she were guarding some secret of Sand Castle Key. And I didn't think it had anything at all to do with *creatures.*

CHAPTER 4

The Wreck of the *San Marcos*

At the library a poster caught my eye. "Look at this," I said, and I read from the poster. *Friday 8 P.M. Captain Scott Ericson, marine archeologist, will talk about the* San Marcos, *the sunken Spanish galleon found off Sand Castle Key.*

Under the poster was a glass exhibit showing pieces of broken pottery, a rusted gun, and some coins—just like mine! All of them had dates from the early seventeen hundreds.

"I bet my coin is from the *San Marcos,*" I whispered.

"It says here that the *San Marcos* sank in 1720." Tim read from a sign in the exhibit: *The museum is working with a recovery ship to bring up artifacts. Each day two different crew members go down to the wreck and send up a basket full of objects they find. Then the items are catalogued and appraised for their values.*

"That must be the boat we saw from the island," said Denise.

Melissa was studying photographs of the recovery crew. "There's the lady we met on the beach." Sure enough, there she was, right in the midst of the crew. "No wonder she knew about the coelacanth. She's a scientist. Her name is Dr. Lynn Stokes."

"Another reason to believe her when she talked about that sea creature," said Denise.

When we got back to the retirement park, Grandpa was out in his workshop. "Grandpa!" I yelled. "We found some really neat fossils on Sand Castle Key."

"Let's take a look." Grandpa cleared off some space on his workbench and spread out the contents of our pails. "Nice collection," he said, as he held up a rock. "See this piece? It's the vertebra of a whale or dolphin, I believe. As the bone decayed in the sand, each of its tiny cells slowly filled with minerals until finally, the bone was gone, leaving an exact replica in stone."

"Petrification," said Cassie, with an I-told-you-so grin aimed at Tim.

"Look at this rock," Grandpa went on. "You can see the shape of a shell. The original shell decayed and left this space, called a mold." Grandpa touched Cassie's broken arm. "Your cast is like a mold. When your cast comes off, you will see the exact shape of your arm hollowed out."

"Once I identify all these fossils, I'll be finished with my homework," I said. "Then the Geckos have another project."

"What's that?" asked Grandma, who had just joined us.

I showed them the black coin. "I found this out on Sand Castle Key."

Grandpa took the coin and looked it over. "This looks like an old Spanish piece."

"They have some just like it at the library. They're next to a poster about tomorrow night's lecture on the sunken ship," I told him.

"Josh found it washed up among the shells," Tim added.

"That's how the ship was discovered," Grandma explained. "That Spanish galleon has been buried in the sand for centuries. When the hurricane struck, it changed the shoreline and stirred up the sand. Then coins were discovered on the beach."

"This coin is probably not worth a lot as silver, but it might have some value as a historical piece," Grandpa said. "Let's clean it off and see whether we can find a date."

Grandma handed him a jar of silver polish, and Grandpa gently buffed the coin with a rag. The cloth turned black with tarnish, but slowly, the coin began to take on a sheen. The cross on the one side was clear now. And on the other side was a shield with the words *PHILIP V.*

"The King of Spain," Grandma said.

"There's a date!" Cassie pointed. "1715!"

Grandpa handed me the coin. "You should take this down to the library lecture tomorrow night and have it properly identified."

I pocketed the silver piece. "If people find out about this, everyone will come out to the island and we'll never find any more."

Grandpa nodded. "You may be right, but most folks went out to search Sand Castle Key when the wreck was first discovered."

"They didn't find much," Grandma added, "and after they heard most people found old cannons or broken dishes, they lost interest."

"No jewels or gold?" I must have looked disappointed, because Grandma put her arm around me.

"No treasure, Joshua," she said. "But don't feel bad. You did find that wonderful coin."

"I think the Geckos should forget the rumors about the creatures and search Sand Castle Key once more," I said.

Grandma looked worried. "If you do go tomorrow, be sure to check the tides first. And I'll feel a lot better if you bring our cell phone with you."

"I think the Geckos are on the brink of a discovery," said Cassie.

Denise's voice trembled. "I just hope..."

"...that it's not some scary sea creature," her twin concluded.

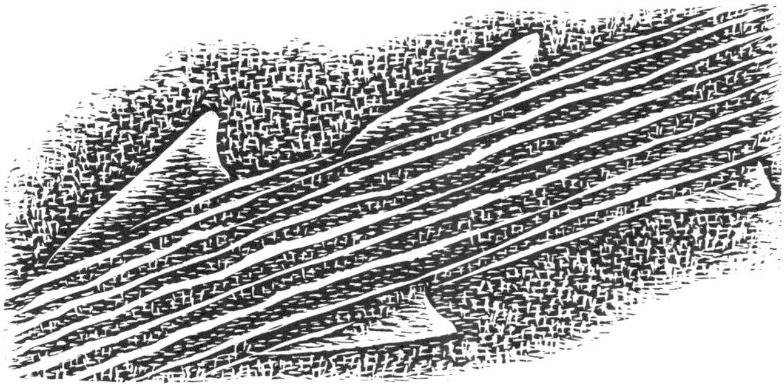

CHAPTER 5
Terrifying Tracks!

That night I finished my science project. I identified all my fossils from the library book. Then I put them in neat boxes. Most of my fossils were shells and sharks' teeth plus some whale and dolphin vertebrae. I wished I had found a mastodon tooth or saber-toothed cat fang. Still, I had a nice collection. "I think I'll get an A," I said confidently.

"You've done a fantastic job," Grandma agreed, as she looked over my display.

"Fossils help us know what the world was like long ago," said Grandpa. "We have an abundance of fossils here. Each time there's a storm, more fossils are dug up by the waves."

“The word *fossil* means ‘dug up’,” I said, feeling like a real paleontologist.

Friday morning I checked the newspaper for the tides. The next low tide wasn’t until 11 A.M. I called the Geckos and we decided to meet at the pavilion at eleven o’clock.

Cassie showed up with a big grin carrying her cast under her arm. “The doctor took it off this morning,” she explained. “I asked him to let me keep this half.” She sat down and filled her old cast with sand. “Now my cast has become a mold,” she said. When the cast was full, she turned it onto the sand, patted it, and then carefully removed it. On the beach was a perfect copy of Cassie’s arm—from above the elbow down to the wrist!

“Neat!” I laughed. “It looks like a one-armed creature crawled onto the sand.”

Cassie got up and dumped the cast into a trash can. “Good riddance!”

We walked to the end of the island and crossed the shallow moat to Sand Castle Key. Clouds had gathered and the sky was dark. I was glad I had Grandma’s phone in my pack.

"We've got to work fast," I said. "We don't want to be stranded on the beach if there's lightning."

I looked out to sea and spotted the recovery ship. A smaller motor boat was leaving with members of the crew.

"I heard the crew goes to shore for supplies every week," Denise explained.

"And tonight is Captain Ericson's lecture at the library," Melissa added.

"He probably needs a shower," said Tim. Everyone burst out laughing.

We headed for the midden where I found the silver coin and then stopped suddenly. Tim pointed to the sand. "There are those creepy tracks again."

"It's something with fins and claws," Cassie exclaimed. "Let's follow them!"

Melissa crossed her arms. "Not me!"

"We came to find coins, not creatures!" her sister said.

But Cassie was mounting the midden and after a moment, we all ran after her. The tracks disappeared into the midden shells.

By now the sky was really black, and it was beginning to rain. Denise pointed to the weather-beaten fishing shack. "Let's go inside until it stops raining."

The fishing shack had two rooms with no windows. We could hear the rain beating down and dripping through the holes in the roof. *Crash!* Lightning streaked across the sky. Tim peered out of the cracks in the boards. "It's like night out there. Wait a minute—" His voice lowered to a frightened whisper. "Something is crawling out of the water and onto the beach!"

Terrified, we peeked through the slats. At first all we saw were shadows, but in a flash of lightning we could see—two scuba divers! They were dragging a metal basket out from the surf. The basket seemed to be full of junk and seaweed.

"They're heading this way," said Cassie. "What shall we say if they find us?"

"We'll tell them we've come in here to get out of the storm," I said. Still, it was scary watching those two figures in black dragging that metal basket. "Their fins and the sharp edges of the basket are what made those tracks," I said softly.

They were closer now and we could hear the sounds of the basket scraping against the shells of the midden. The two divers staggered to the embankment and then stopped.

A man's voice called out, "I'll get the shovel in the shack."

We ran to the back room.

The man found a shovel near the door and went back outside. We could hear him digging. We moved to the other wall and peered out through the cracks. The two divers had uncovered a plastic cooler. They emptied the contents of the bucket into the cooler and then covered it again with sand and shells.

Lightning flashed and a clap of thunder rumbled.

The other diver spoke, "Maybe we should stay in the shack until the storm ends." It was a woman's voice! Where had I heard it before?

We huddled together, trembling. These people were up to no good. What would happen if they found us?

The door banged. Now the divers were in the next room! Cautiously, I peeked through a knothole in the wall. The woman had pulled back her mask. It was Lynn Stokes, the lady from the beach!

"We should get going, Jim," she said.

"The storm's almost over, and those kids may be back."

Jim uncovered his face. He looked like one of the crew members in the library photograph. "I thought you scared them off."

"I tried, but they were a curious bunch. I think they found something out here besides fossils," she said. "You've got to be more careful when you drag that basket. Something may have fallen out."

"Don't complain. I'm only human." Jim's voice rose. "When we find the good stuff at the wreck, *I'm* the one who takes it off to another spot until we can bring it to shore."

"Well, I cover for you," Lynn snapped. "If it weren't for me, the crew would wonder what was going on. While you're hiding the good artifacts, I send up the less valuable objects to the ship."

"It makes me nervous, swimming in here, hoping there's no one around, or waiting until the crew goes to port," Jim complained.

"Come at night if you're so worried. You used to do that."

"I have to use a flashlight then. And now people are talking about lights out here in the middle of the night."

"Well, one more day and we're out of here," said Lynn.

"The rain's slowing down. Let's go," said Jim. The two divers left the shack.

At that moment the phone in my backpack began to ring!

CHAPTER 6
Gifts from the Past

I yanked off my backpack and fumbled with the zipper. The phone rang again!

"Turn it off!" Tim murmured.

Cassie was watching the divers. "It's okay. They didn't hear it."

"Hello?" I whispered into the phone.

"It's Grandma. Are you all right? When the storm struck, we began to worry. Why are you whispering?"

"Listen carefully, Grandma." I told the entire story about Dr. Lynn Stokes and the man she called Jim burying loot on the island. "They've been stealing from the sunken ship and hiding the treasures out here."

Grandpa was on the extension. "Get out of there, quickly," he said. "I'll tell the police and we'll meet you at Manasota Key."

I hung up, relieved that Grandpa was getting help.

"We've got to get out of here," I said, and we headed out the door.

But Cassie grabbed the shovel. "Let's see what's in that cooler."

"No!" Denise said. "They may come back."

Cassie ignored her and handed me the shovel. I knew better than to argue with Cassie. I started digging, and it wasn't long until we uncovered the plastic cooler.

Tim reached down and pulled at the cover until it popped open. We stood back with our eyes bugging out. Inside the chest was a cache of jewelry and gold objects.

"Look at this!" Cassie pulled out a necklace with sparkling blue gems.

"A sword scabbard!" Tim drew the jewel-encrusted sheath from the box.

"Lots of gold coins and silver, like mine," I said. Some pieces needed to be polished, or were damaged, but I knew they were valuable. "It sounded like those two divers will be coming back soon to take all this away," I said.

"So now what do we do?" asked Tim.

"This cooler is too heavy to carry all the way back," I said, "but we can bury it somewhere else until we get help."

"Let's take some of the pieces to show to the authorities, so they'll believe us," Cassie suggested. I took off my backpack, and Cassie put some coins and the necklace into one of the pockets.

"Let's bury the cooler down by that palm tree," said Tim. We took turns digging a hole. Then we dragged the cooler down, buried it, and scattered shells and sand over it.

"We've got to get back fast," I said. "Those two crooks may show up at any time."

We had only gone a short way up the beach when I looked back. The divers had come out of the water again! After watching us for a moment, they kicked off their flippers and ran up the midden to where they had buried the cooler.

"Run!" I yelled. "They're looking for the treasure."

Now we could hear Jim yelling at us. "Come back here!"

"They know we've moved their stash," Denise whimpered.

The divers darted after us. "Run!" Cassie screamed.

When we reached the moat, we leaped into the water. We tried to run, but the water was up to our waists now and the current was strong from the storm.

"Stop!" yelled Lynn. They were catching up to us.

On the other side of the moat, I could see the flashing lights of police cars—and Grandpa waving us on. "Come on," he yelled. "You can make it!"

Although the water made it hard for us to run, we kept moving as fast as we could. Grandpa and a police officer waded in and helped us onto the beach.

Back on Sand Castle Key, Lynn Stokes and her companion had turned around and were racing in the other direction.

We could hear the clapping of a police helicopter overhead. As it landed on Sand Castle Key, Lynn and her accomplice raced for the water, but two police officers jumped out of the helicopter and pulled them from the waves.

Later, the Geckos got to ride in the helicopter out to the island to recover the stolen treasure.

That night, at the library, Captain Ericson gave his speech. Then he called the Geckos up to the podium.

"The *San Marcos* lost its treasure to a storm. Today we found out that the most valuable museum pieces were almost lost again, because of greed. Thanks to the Geckos, this didn't happen," he said. "We want to show our appreciation by giving you a gift from the past."

It was awesome! Captain Ericson presented a shiny gold doubloon from the treasure to each of us.

Denise whispered, "Let's have these made into..."

"...necklaces!" said her twin.

"Super!" Cassie agreed.

Tim and I looked at each other. A gold necklace with a real Spanish doubloon was a great idea.

The Geckos made the eleven o'clock news, and the morning headlines read:

KIDS SAVE ANCIENT TREASURE!

There we were, right on the front page, grinning and holding up our gold pieces.

The article explained how Dr. Stokes and her accomplice stole the most valuable artifacts, planning to sell them to collectors around the world.

The paper credited the Geckos for saving the treasure and solving the mystery of the creatures on Sand Castle Key.

The next day we sat on the beach basking in the sun, feeling like celebrities.

Cassie sighed. "I wonder what kind of mystery we'll solve on our next vacation."

Melissa answered, "We've had enough mysteries to last..."

"...a long, long time," Denise finished.

"Come on, let's go swimming!" Cassie yelled, running to the surf. "And watch out for *CREATURES!"*

As we dashed after Cassie, I yelled out, "You know, it's all thanks to me and my homework assignment that we solved this mystery!"

"Sure, take all the credit," said Tim with a wicked grin at the girls.

SPLASH!

The Geckos dunked me in the waves!